The Unknown Ethnic Cleansings

White Spots in Modern History

S. WARGIN

BALBOA.
PRESS

A DIVISION OF HAY HOUSE

Balboa Press books may be ordered through booksellers or by contacting:

Balboa Press
A Division of Hay House
1663 Liberty Drive
Bloomington, IN 47403
www.balboapress.com.au
1 (877) 407-4847

Print information available on the last page.

ISBN: 978-1-5043-0375-0 (sc)
ISBN: 978-1-5043-0376-7 (e)

Balboa Press rev. date: 08/24/2016

Contents

Chapter 1

In the Middle Ages, the sparsely populated lands east of the Polish kingdom were a constant bone of contention for the governments of Poland, Russia, and Turkey and, therefore, the cause of numerous wars. The lands *u kraju,* at the eastern edge of Poland, could be compared with the Wild West of the American colonies. Mostly out of reach of the institutions of law and order, this was a place of refuge for those in trouble with the powers that be and their laws. From u kraju the name of these lands became known as Ukraine.

The sparse popluation consisted of Russian-speaking peasants. The culture was barely more advanced then those living in the Stone Age. There were some fortified settlements of Polish and other gentry. Besides serving as a refuge for those in serious trouble with the law, it was a thoroughfare for countless attacks and quick raids into the more settled and wealthier towns and settlements of central and western Poland. These raids were carried out by various marauding tribes of Tartars, Turks, and others.

German tribes to the west subscribed to the principle of *Drang nach Osten* (expansion to the east by force or guile). Therefore, alliances with neighbouring kingdoms became a political necessity for Poland.

After several alliances with the neighbouring pagan kingdom of Lithuania, a permanent union of the two kingdoms was achieved with the 1385 marriage of Prince Jagiello of Lithuania to Queen Jadwiga of Poland. The subsequent adoption of the Catholic religion by the prince and his kingdom further solidified the alliance. Now united, the two kingdoms effectively stopped the expansion of the German tribes under the leadership of the German Knights Order during the victorious battle of Grunwald in 1410. They were also successful in curtailing Russian and Turkish expansion efforts to the west. As a result, the Polish development of the lands now proceeded. These towns and villages with a mixed population became subject to the rule of the United Kingdom.

Polish nobility and the Catholic Church became the bearers of culture into a primitive land with a mixed population of illiterate peasants of pagan, Orthodox, Muslim, and Jewish beliefs. In the towns and castles the Cossacks were placed between the nobility and the peasants.

Those with ambition were eager to become part of the nobility by any means necessary. Their sons obtained education at the Jesuit college at Lwow. Among the pupils there was a Bochdan Zenobi Chmielnicki, the son of an official of the local law court. He realised that the peasants had no chance to join the ranks of the nobility. In the Cossacks, he saw an ally in the struggle to raise his social status. Chmielnicki, as a local landowner and Cossack, decided to exploit the peasants to become a local lord, create his own state, or force the United Kingdom to include him in its ruling class. In the spring of 1648, he instigated a peasant uprising in the Ukraine with initial successes against the United Kingdom. However, the kingdom rallied and defeated him in 1651 in the battle near the town of Beresteczko. Having failed, he looked for a powerful ally in the Russian czar who, in 1654, placed the Ukraine under his rule.

At that time, the concept of a distinct Ukrainian national identity was unknown. There was no such kingdom or principality. The Tartars of the Crimean Peninsula ceased their support of Chmielnicki. For them, Russia was a more dangerous opponent than the United Kingdom. Chmielnicki, in his efforts to obtain some sort of autonomy, reached out to Sweden and Berlin for support. Under the czar's reign, there was a determined effort to de-Polonize Ukraine in favour of the national consciousness of the Lithuanian and Ukrainian peasantry. There was a constant increase of the Jewish influence in commerce and trade.

After the partition of Poland by the three superpowers of the time—Prussia, Austria, and Russia—between the years 1772 and 1795, a great number of Jews settled in that area. At that time, the region was called Ukraine and was part of the Russian empire. The south eastern area of Poland was incorporated into the Austro-Hungarian empire and was called by Austria Galicja, administered according to the principle of divide and rule of the mixed population. The Austro-Hungarian empire supported the development of Ukrainian nationalism, claiming even Ruthenians or Ruthenes as Ukrainians.

In the twentieth century, a section of the population there started to call themselves Ukrainians. Being primitive, illiterate peasants, they resented the Latin culture of the Poles. The Ukrainians wanted to name Lwow their capital. According to Austrian records, 175,560 people spoke Polish as their mother tongue, 21,780 spoke Ukrainian, and a great number of Jews spoke Yiddish there.

The influential Jewish population set up their political parties, the oldest being the *Algemeiner Judischer Arbeiter Bund* (the Bund) in Wilno in 1897. The Bund Party strenuously opposed an independent Poland. In World War I (WWI), it supported the establishment of a Jewish homeland in the territories in the east (including Ukraine) that were conquered by Germany. Austria, in the part of Poland they incorporated into their empire, sent conscripted Poles to the Italian front. They kept some twelve thousand conscripted Ukrainians in what they named Galicja.

When it became obvious that Germany was about to lose the war, Jewish efforts changed direction. At that time the known personality in Paris of the emerging Polish state was count Orlowski. On the 11.11.1918 he had a visit from the well- known Jewish financier Morris Rothschild who threatened that the Jews would block any attempt by the emerging Polish state to regain Danzig, Silezia, Lwow (Lemberg) and Wilno if the representative of Poland at the Versailles peace conference will be the popular Polish statesman and nationalist Roman Dmowski. They sought to force Poland to give special privileges to any minorities on its territory. Defeated Germany supported any local settlers and religions there that were hostile to the emerging Polish state. A mob of Ukrainian peasants under the leadership of an Austrian Jewish captain by the name Eisler, and supported by agitators from the ranks of the Ukrainian Greek Catholic church and Ukrainian conscrips stationed there, attempted to size the Polish city of Lwow (now renamed Lemberg by the Austrians) for a Ukrainian government created by Germany.

The population of that city, 80 per cent of whom were of Polish descent, valiantly defended the city. On November 22, 1919, they were relieved by the Polish Army. Some 6,022 people fought in the defence of Lwow, including primary- and secondary-school students. The youngest was just nine years old; none of the defenders were over the age of twenty five. In all, 439 people—including 12 women, 120 pupils, and 76 students—died. To get weapons, they had to storm an Austrian armoury from where they obtained rifles and ammunition.

Polish defence headquarters staff in Lwow 1919 (in public domain).

CiC Polish defence of Lwow Czeslaw Maczynski (in public domain).

After the armed forces of the emerging Polish state defeated the Bolshevik army's goals to drive westward and spread their ideology to Germany in 1920, Ukraine became again part of sovereign Poland. Disloyalty by minorities was supported by the neighbours from both east and west and by the Greek Catholic Church, the cradle of Ukrainian nationalism. In 1922, of 683 Greek Catholic priests in the diocese of Stanislawow, as many as 571 displayed a disloyal attitude to the Polish state (*Catholic News Warsaw* July 9, 1989). In the south-eastern border regions of Poland, there were no obvious and permanent political, cultural, and ethnic borders.

In 1931, the use of the Polish language in the various border districts was as follows.

Wilno: 59.7 per cent
Nowogrod: 52 per cent
Polesie: 14.5 per cent
Wolyn: 16.6 per cent
Tarnopol: 49.3 per cent
Stanislawow: 22.4 per cent
Lwow: 57.7 per cent

By 1939, the total population of these areas was thirteen million. It consisted of the following subpopulations.

Poles: 43 per cent
Ukrainians: 33 per cent
Jews: 8.3 per cent
All others: 13.7 per cent

In August 1939, as the consequence of an agreement between the German Abwehr (intelligence agency) and leading Ukrainian nationalists, a legion of two battalions, the Nachtigall and the

Roland, was formed. In addition, before the German invasion, a Ukrainian legion of a thousand men under the leadership of Colonel Roman Suszki underwent training in Germany. This force became part of the Fourteenth Field Army under the command of General List during the German invasion.

Dmytro Witowski (1877–1919), one of the leaders
of the assault on Lwow (in public domain).

The Nachtigall Battalion took part in the ethnic cleansing of Poles and Jews in the cities of Lwow, Satanowo, Winnica, Zloczow, Tarnopol, and Proskurow. A punishment unit, it consisted of professional criminals known for their extreme cruelty. The Roland Battalion, formed in February 1941, moved to Romania under the command of an army group with 9 officers and 260 men. The unit was again transferred to Neuhammer, Germany, merged with the Nachtigall Battalion, and formed the 201 Schutzmannschaft (security guards) battalion.

Poland 1939

Chapter 2

At the same time that Germany made unacceptable demands on Poland, Ukrainian commandos were located in eastern Poland to cause an uprising and sabotage. They prepared a list of local Polish notables for elimination. Beginning on September 10,1939 Ukrainian deserters from the Polish army appeared in eastern Poland to form their own units. German authorities, however, did not initially give the order for an uprising, and when it was finally given, it was too late.

In September, Ukrainian militias attacked Polish villages. Twelve villagers died in Grabow. Locals and refugees from western Poland died in Lesniaki, Zapole, and Kniahinek. In November, two hundred refugees from central Poland were murdered by Ukrainian peasants at Nawoz. After the Soviet invasion of eastern Poland in accordance with the Ribbentrop–Molotov pact of August 23, 1939, those territories were occupied by the Soviet Union. In some townships where there was no police left, drags of Ukrainian society formed militias, displaying red armbands in order to enrich themselves on Polish property. After the 1941 invasion of the Soviet Union by Germany, eastern Poland became part of the German-occupied Soviet Union.

Since the beginning of time, superpowers Germany and Russia made strenuous and often successful attempts to include those territories and its various ethnic groups into the own cultural sphere at the expense of the influential Polish and Catholic cultures. After the outbreak of WW II, there was no restraint in the ethnic cleansing of these territories by the minorities of Ukrainians, Baltics, and Germans. All, of course, saw their minorities as faithful allies of the Reich and despised by it as *Hiwis, Hilfswillige,* meaning those willing to assist in the creation of the one-thousand-year Reich. One of the heroes they created was the Ukrainian peasant who adopted the name of Taras Bulba after the invasion of the USSR by Germany. His real name was Maksym Tarae Borowec. His formal education consisted of four classes at a public school.

As an expression of gratitude to Hitler, Ukrainians erected welcoming gates and signs seen by witnesses July 6, 1941, at Woronczyn and many other places. At the same time, steps of ethnic cleansing were taken with the murder of four Poles on the June 28, 1941, at Olganowka Nowa; the murder of two inhabitants of a nearby village on July 1; and on July 2 in Retowo, the murder of Jan Pachle, who was married to a Ukrainian woman. On July 4, at the settlement of Sitarowka, three Poles and one Jew were murdered. In the same month, at Michalin, a Polish air force lieutenant was murdered.

The head of the Greek Catholic Church, Archbishop A. Szeptyckij, issued three pastoral letters of thanks to the Reich and recommended prayers for victory. He gave his support to the nationalist government created in Lwow and was appointed president of the Ukrainian National Council (URN). This was done without obtaining German approval, and in a couple of days, caused a reaction. Almost all were arrested, and Stepan

Bandera, the chief of a section of the OUN (Organisation of Ukrainian Nationalists) and son of a Catholic Orthodox priest, was sent to the Sachsenhausen concentration camp.

Ukrainian nationalism, the *motorum motivabum* of the ethnic cleansing, has its roots in the support given in the nineteenth century by the Austrian empire that occupied that part of Poland and endeavoured to reduce Polish cultural influence by favouring other ethnic groups in that region. The Catholic Orthodox Church, quite strong and influential in that region, supported Ukrainian nationalism against Latin Catholicism; many of their clergy were leaders of that movement. The celibate obligation—as evidenced by Bandera's father, who was a priest—of the Roman Catholic Church, did not to this day apply to them. During Hitler's rule of the Reich, Dmytro Doncow translated Hitler's book *Mein Kampf* into Ukrainian for those who could read.

After every massacre of the Polish population in villages and towns, Ukrainian women and children arrived on horse-drawn carriages to plunder the homes of the sadistically killed inhabitants before they were put to the torch. These actions erased any trace that Poles lived there for centuries.

Poles massacred at Lipniki (in public domain).
Copyright by publisher Nortom, Wroclaw, Poland.

Ukrainian police commander of Podhorce, initiator and
participant of the Huta Piernacka massacre.
Copyright by Norton publisher, Wroclaw, Poland.

Poland Today

Note the area enclosed by dots, which was stolen by her neighbours. It is an arca of 18,000 square kilometres with a population of 13 million.

The attitude of the leadership of the Reich was different to states deemed to be their allies as compared to occupied territories where different ethnic groups tried to create their own states. While winning the war on the eastern front, they did not encourage the development of any new states. They went so far as to jail known nationalist agitators, such as Bandera and others in the Ukraine. However, after Stalingrad on February 2, 1943, and Kursk on July 16, 1943, the heavy drain on the manpower reserves of the Reich, the ever-increasing resistance, and the underground activities in the occupied territories demanded a watering down of the ideology for practical reasons. Not many were willing to end up on the eastern front. Nationalist activists were set free to reorganise their own militias with the material and instructional help of the occupying power.

The ancient hostility between the ethnic groups was to be exploited to keep the supply of manpower and material to the frontl safe and rolling according to the motto, *Rader mussen rollen fur den Sieg,* ("Wheels must roll for victory"). Cynics added to that slogan the words. *Kinderwagen fur den nachsten Krieg* ("Prams for the next war").

The role of guarding the supply lines and the suppression of hostile partisan units was given to the militias. Those minorities in occupied countries that claimed, rightly or wrongly, to have been discriminated against by the pre-war regimes there were promised independence and a chance to clear the areas they lived in of other nationalities; that is, ethnic cleansing.

The more primitive they were, the easier they could be moulded to serve the German war effort. Eastern Poland was soon full of militias such as the UPA (Ukrainian Insurrection Army, established autumn 1942), OUN, the Bandera group, and others. They acted primarily in their own interests when the circumstances were suitable: to clear eastern Poland of Poles and Jews in order to create a Ukrainian state. Their favourite targets were defenceless villages of the Polish population and any others who did not assist the militias. They were to be killed in the most sadistic way to make those territories Ukrainian. One of the first major actions of ethnic cleansing of the Polish population by the UPA occurred on February 9, 1943, in the village Parosle in the Sarnenski district in German-occupied eastern Poland. In the action, 173 Poles were butchered. Under German control, a Ukrainian police force was set up and appropriately armed. Once trained and armed, they switched over to the UPA, and on the night of April 22 and 23, they attacked the settlement of Janowa Dolina, killing six hundred Poles.

Partisans of the Polish AK and NSZ endeavoured to counteract the cleansing. As a result, the population that escaped left their ancient lands and moved westward for a little more safety. With full agreement of the German occupying powers, the ethnic cleansing of the Polish population by the various Ukrainian militias got underway in 1943. On July 11 of that year, fifty-two worshippers were killed in the church at Poryck.

Children butchered by the UPA.
Copyright by Norton publisher, Wroclaw, Poland.

Graduates of a Ukrainian seminary that volunteered for SS Galizien.
Copyright by Norton publishers Wroclaw, Poland.

Chapter 3

The same day as the massacre at Poryck took place, a church service at Kisielin was attacked, and 180 worshippers and the priest killed. In August, the villages of Ostrowka and Wola Ostrowiecka were attacked and over a thousand inhabitants killed, including four hundred children. The following villages were attacked and put to the torch with considerable loss of life: Baligrod, Muczem, Sakowczyk, Cisna, Tworylne, Dylagowa, Nowotanic, Orzechow, Bricz, Strzembowisk, Borownica, Krzywe, Temeszow, Prusiek, Leszczowate, Berlikow, Ropienka, Wankowa, Wola Michowa, Wola Sekowa, Siemuzowa, Krylowe. In the Wolyn district, Dubno lost 1,900, Horochow 2,400, Kostopolska 4,400, Kowel 3,350, and Krzemienic 3,000. The elimination of the Polish population there was not only planned by the Ukrainian leadership during World War two. Already in the 1926 book by Dmytr Doncow of the title 'Nationalism' the author hints what to do there with those that are not Ukrainians. "National fanatism is the weapon of strong nations by which great deeds are done". Roman Szuchewycz, the 1943 leader of the UPA instructed Ukrainians to treat Jews the same as Poles and Roma, not sparing any (prof.E.Prus 'The Bandera Holocaust' London 1992).

The Polish population was not prepared or warned of the approaching ethnic cleansing unhindered by the occupiers. The mass killings of the Polish population of the Wolyn district was carried out on February 9, 1943, in the village of Parosla; 173 were killed. In the city of Lwow, the Bandera group murdered some three thousand Poles and Jews right after the city was occupied by the Germans. The reaction of the so-called educated class (educated in Hitler's Germany) of the western Ukraine was and is to blame the victims whose ancestors settled in the then great emptiness some six hundred or fewer years ago; it is not the perpetrator's fault. An UPA detachment commanded by Roman Szuchewycz carried out ethnic cleansing action in Podkamien (150 victims), Brynce Zagorne (140 victims), and Berezowica Mala (135 victims). Survivors endeavoured to go westward to settlements that had a German military presence for some safety.

The killing of Poles was greatly increased after the Ukarinian police, in the service of the occupier, joined the UPA. During a reception by the governor Hans Frank of the Generalgovernment Polen of the 5.3.1940 at Cracow Frank admitted that he had problems with the Polish underground. He said to solve that problem we will have the help of 600 000 Ukrainians the enemies from the cradle of anything Polish (prof. E. Prus 'Bluff of the XX Century' London) As mentioned previously, in the night of April 22–23, the settlement of Janowa Dolina was put to the torch and six hundred killed. The killing was carried out in a way as to inflict maximum suffering to the victims, according to Col. Jan Niewinski who, with a group of Polish partisans, defended the village of Rybcza against the UPA and local Ukrainians.

Andrew Szeptyckij, Greek Catholic archbishop of Lwow.
Copyright by Norton publisher, Wroclaw, Poland.

Various Ukrainian militia groups led by professional criminals attacked Poles living in villages, killing and plundering. This was the fate of Poles in Parosla (150 killed), Janowa Dolina (600 killed), Ostrowki (476 killed), and Wola Ostrowiecka (572 killed). Even at the end of WW II, ethnic cleansing of the Polish population occurred in the Puzniki district Buczacz in the Tarnopol region by Greek-Catholic Ukrainians on the order of OUN.

1. Borkowska, Maria   shot
2. Borkowski, Jozef   bayonetted
3. Guzowaski, Jozef   incinerated
4. Janiska, Danicela   burnt alive

5. Jasinska, Maria	bayonetted
6. Jasinska, Wladyslawa	garrotted
7. Jasinski, Jozef	killed with sledge hammer
8. Jerzycka, Stainslawa	shot
9. Krzywon, Aloizy	killed with hammer
Kulikowska, Genowefa	garrotted
10. Kuliszczak, Jan	killed with hammer
11. Kuliszczak, Jozefa	killed with hammer
12. Kwiatek, Jozef	shot
13. Lopiak, Anastazia	burnt alive
14. Lopiak, Kazimiera	burnt alive
15. Rola, Jozefa	killed with sledge hammer
16. Rola, Mieczyslaw	shot
17. Rola, Stanislawa	killed with sledge hammer
18. Suchecka, Maria	killed with sledge hammer
19. Tyc, Jozef	burnt alive
20. Winsiewska, Rozalia	killed with sledge hammer
21. Wisniewski, Zbigniew	bayonetted

A local, Alexander Praduna, was an eyewitness to the UPA massacre of the adjacent villages of Ostrowka and Wola Ostrowieka in the Wolyn district. Men, women, children, and infants were forced to assemble in an empty field. Each of the killers grabbed a handful of victims and forced them to lie down to be shot. Mothers took their children in their arms. The killers were poor shots, and the victims did not die instantly but died slowly, bludgeoned by rifle butts. Praduna saw a little girl of about six years old who, after being shot, got up and screamed, "Mother, mother, mother!" But her mother was already dead. The Ukrainian shot her three more times, but the bullets did not kill her. Finally, he resorted to hitting her with his rifle butt.

A report by the AK (Polish Home Army) of the Tarnopol region states that from August 1943 to January 1944, Ukrainians murdered 1,101 Poles in that area alone. On June 16, 1943, a UPA unit dressed in German uniforms stopped a train, consisting of a locomotive and one carriage, travelling between Bellzca towards Rawa Ruska in the middle of a field; the Ukrainian driver of the train was a collaborator. There were some seventy Poles—men women, and children on the train. They were removed from the train and shot in the nearby field.

Ukrainians collaborated with both Hitler's armies and the Communists as long as they were allowed to kill Poles. Decapitation by a sickle and cutting open the bellies of pregnant women was not unusual. Nor were the sadistic killings of children by dismemberment. The village of Pendyki was razed in March 1943, and around 150 inhabitants were killed.

Victims of the UPA attack on the train at
Lubycza Krolewska June 16, 1944.
Copyright by Norton publisher, Wroclaw, Poland.

Admission to the outside world of these barbaric ethnic cleansing actions among Ukrainian notables is as rare as hen's teeth. An exception was Leonid Markarowych Krachu, president of the Ukraine 1991–1994. In one of his speeches, he admitted, In WW II Ukrainian chauvinists killed some half a million of Poles in eastern pre-war Poland."

This booklet gives only a few examples. There are not enough pages in this book to mention all the localities and medieval atrocities perpetrated there. It only shows that the mentality of west Ukrainians has not undergone any changes in this century despite the constant propaganda to the contrary. Even if there are no witnesses, wholesale ethnic cleansing was carried out on any majority or minority that did not support a state brought into existence as an ally of National Socialist Germany and a provider of auxiliaries for the Wehrmacht. After ethnic cleansing, the villages were utterly destroyed. No traces were left to remind the casual traveller that this was once part of Poland.

Volunteers for the SS Galizien.
Copyright by Norton publisher, Wroclaw, Poland

Chapter 4

Most educated people in the Anglo-Saxon world have heard of the SS that carried out the ethnic cleansing of the Jews in German and territories it occupied during WW II. Most will not be aware of other nations that suffered the same fate (except a handful of homosexuals and Roma) because the mass media worldwide is in the hands of a few moguls, and only what they want the public to know is published. That is their understanding of the freedom of the press.

After the heavy losses by the Wehrmacht at Stalingrad and Kursk, the powers that be decided to water down temporarily their racial guidelines and use minorities in occupied lands to shore up the heavy losses of manpower for the Wehrmacht. Nationalist activists were released from jails and concentration camps to organise auxiliary troops for the depleted Wehrmacht. On March 4, 1943, Dr. Wachter, governor of the occupied region of Poland called Galizien, proposed to the Reichsfuhrer Himmler of the SS the formation of a volunteer division from suitable men living as the miniority in West Ukraine. This proposal was supported by Professor Kubiyvich of the Ukrainian Central Committee. Of the 800,000 who reported, some 50,000 were deemed suitable. They joined for a variety of reasons, including to avoid being sent to Germany to work in the armament industry, to be trained in weaponry in order to join the UPA militia and cleanse that area of its Polish majority and acquire their properties, or simply to have a better life. They had to swear an oath of allegiance to Hitler and were supported by the Ukrainian Catholic Church. Ethnic cleansing of the Polish population was frequently started on Ukrainian holidays and was preceded by the priests blessing of their weapons, such as axes, pitchforks sickles, and firearms.

The Ukrainian Legion, a small Ukrainian unit raised and trained in Germany, took part in the invasion of Poland in September 1939. The Greek-Catholic Church of the Ukraine expressed its support for German aggression in the words of Bishop Josyf Slipyj, later elevated to cardinal, and in a more discreet form by the primate of that church, Adrzej Szeptyckij. Priests from Ukrainian village parishes actively supported from the pulpit the creation of an SS volunteer Ukrainian division. The presence of priests was unusual in the Waffen SS it was on insistence of the Ukrainian church authorities. There were even incidents where their priests personally participated in the slaughter, such as in the village of Polowce, district of Czortkow, where twenty-two Poles and ten Ukrainians married to Polish women were killed.

Volunteer recruits of SS Galizien swear allegiance to Hitler.
Copyright by Norton publisher, Wroclaw, Poland.

Their superior was Dr. Wasyl Laba, appointed by the head of the church. Attached to the SS Galizien division was a cadet unit to provide future officers and NCOs. In the small town of Podkamien, the population of which was 70 per cent Polish, there was a Marian sanctuary and a Dominican cloister from the fourteenth century. The cloister was full of refugees from neighbouring villages who fled from the murderous Ukrainian militia, the UPA. Hungarian troops, despite being an ally of Germany, gave the refugees some rifles and grenades for their defence against the Ukrainian militia. Attacked in March 1944 by units of the SS Galicien, this historical place of worship was destroyed and some nine hundred Poles killed. Units of the SS Galizien took part in suppression of the Warshaw uprising.

Following is a list of some well-known villages and small towns that were razed by the SS Galizien with heavy loss of life of their inhabitants to make it exclusively Ukrainian: Borow on February 1, 1944 (300 killed); Huta Brodzka, February 14 (burned and 26 killed); Palikowo on March 12 (362 were killed, including several Jews). Huta Pieniacka was sacked on the February 28, and 1,100 killed, including 20 Jews. Podkamien was sacked on the March 11–15 with loss of life. Hodaczkow Wielki was razed on the April 16 with 862 killed. The massacre there was stopped by a humane German officer.

Next in line for elimination was Huta Werchobudzka on March 22. Fifty houses were put to the torch and four hundred inhabitants killed. One Ukainian police commander of Podhorce was the initiator and participated in the killing. A Polish woman was saved during the massacre by a German NCO who told her to pretend she was dead. The Ukrainians would have killed him if they realised he saved her.

Hanczow was sacked on April 9–10. At Siemanowka, with a population of 2,460, including 5 Jewish families, 32 inhabitants were killed on July 26. Kamionka and Przesieka each lost seven inhabitants on July 21. Szczycyn and Wolka Szczecka, on the same date, lost two hundred each. On September 24, Jamna lost twenty-three, Majdan Nowy twenty-eight, and Majdan Stary sixty-five inhabitants were killed and houses razed.

Even during the retreat of the Wehrmacht, various Ukrainian militias and the Ukrainian SS Galicien did not cease to perform ethnic cleansing of Polish villages wherever an opportunity arose. Berezowica Mala was sacked in the night of February 22 to 23, 1944. Ludwikowka shared the same fate in the night of December 17 to 18 with the loss of some two hundred inhabitants. Toustobaby was razed with the loss of some five hundred in February. In total, forty villages and country towns in that area were destroyed, causing the survivors to flee. All this was done according to the now revered in the Ukraine Dmytro Klaczkiwski (also known as Klym Sawur) who in 1943 issued a secret directive to "kill every Pole in the age group of 16 to 60, should something Polish remain, the Poles will have a claim to our lands'.

The perpetrators of the massacres were not only uniformed militia and from the SS Galizien. After them came hordes of primitive peasants with axes, tomahawks, knives, and pitchforks and keen to satisfy their primitive bloodlust and desire for robbery. Some Belorussians took part in this holocaust. Wladmir Aplewicz exploited the opportunity for power and wealth when the Red Army entered Poland as an ally of Germany in 1939. He organised his own red militia to hunt down individual Polish soldiers, policemen, and inhabitants near the village of Budwola. He is credited with killing by torture of eight persons under the pretext that they took part in the war of 1920 against the Soviet Union. During the ethnic cleansing of the villages of Zofiowko and Hryczowo, Anton Andreszczuk took part and later boasted among his UPA mates of his actions.

Others when in the west attempted to blame somebody else for their crimes. There were killers who openly admitted to their parts in the genocide because they were protected by the powers of the day. In accordance with the Yalta agreements 1,843,222 Poles were evicted from lands in the east of Poland that they farmed and developed for centuries. The remnants of the Polish population of eastern Poland were evicted in the years 1955 to 1959. During the stay of the Polish Anders army in the Middle East, many Jews in the army deserted in Palestine and joined the clandestine Stern gang that fought a guerrilla war against the British mandate authorities there and against the majority Arab population. After the war and the establishment of the state of Israel, they became the ruling junta in that newly created state on Palestinian soil.

On Germany's surrender, members of the Ukrainian SS and their chaplains, keen not to fall into or being delivered to Soviet authorities and executed (this only took place in the first months of Germany's surrender), mixed with those who were forced labourers, *Ostarbeiter*, in Germany in displaced persons' camps. After lengthy medical checks and no checks pertaining to their backgrounds, they immigrated to Canada, the United States, Australia, and the United Kingdom to work as factory fodder and those menial jobs no native-born citizen was willing to do. I personally witnessed at a medical inspection for emigration to Australia of fit men with their blood group tattoos under their armpits; only SS members had those.

After 1945, France recruited former members of the Waffen SS, Ukrainians, and other non-Germans, as well as Germans, for their Foreign Legion for North Africa. The newly created German *Bundeswehr* accepted, after 1961, former members of the SS.

Helena Wolinska (nee Taiga Minda Danielek), the chief military prosecutor in communist Poland, a Jewess born 1919, made a meteoritic career from a lowly lieutenant in the Peoples Army; she takes credit for sixteen executions, including that of General August Fieldorf of the AK. After the war, she received British protection and citizenship. To appease its population, previous Polish authorities tried in vain to extradite the murderess from the United Kingdom to face a lenient Polish court for her crimes.

So much for British justice; no more than only the advantage of the more powerful. Today, UK personnel is sent to the Ukraine to train Ukrainian forces (*Guardian* February 25, 2015) that are based on the tradition of the SS Galicien, UPA, and other butchers of the Polish population of eastern Poland. Their knowledge as to how to inflict maximum pain while killing may have been considered by the powers of the day an asset that could be used in case of the next war.

Australia and the United Kingdom were not far behind in this discriminatory act. On arriving in Australia, Ukrainian chaplains organised a vicious and false propaganda campaign among the Australian clergy in South Australia against anything Polish. So did their educated class that, as allies of Germany, survived the war intact. The late Polish chaplain Father Kuczmanski (a concentration camp survivor) was amazed at the hostility displayed to him by Australian priests when he arrived with his fellow DPs in Adelaide in 1949—until he found out who was behind this hate campaign. The then archbishop of Adelaide Beovich, however, was not fooled by the Ukrainian priests' propaganda campaign and treated the Poles fairly.

The term "democracy" is the most misused term in the mass media, by politicians, and by ordinary citizens. Everyone has their own interpretations of it without ever studying the original Athenian democracy. Under this shield, today your mail can be opened, your phone conversation monitored, your Internet contacts checked, your reading habits from the local library checked, your writing censored and stopped from publication, and your property seized by any government just because a worldwide conglomerate wants to build a supermarket there. When there is a census, you have to answer all personal questions, any refusal will be punished more severely then an ordinary crime. The only difference compared to a dictatorship is that it is done discreetly by the more powerful and, of course, news of it is never published in all the monopolistic media. Money is power, and you, who have less of it, will finally lose. Should you win, you will de facto lose as you will be bankrupt. Opinions that do not follow the official line, whether spoken or written, are not encouraged. Wars of aggression are called wars in defence of the homeland, causing suffering to most and immense wealth to some. It is always the other side that does cruel things; your side is described as knights in shining armour. There is no absolute truth in the media. Truth is relative, according to who says it and whose purpose it serves. Oppressive laws passed by government in times of war or other emergencies are never repealed after the event and can be used by powers that be to stifle any criticism of their actions. Where there is a conflict, the so called neutrals favour the winner, while on the quiet supplying arms, equipment, and food to both sides. A sailor of the *Kriegsmarine* told me the attitude of Swedish authorities to those who were placed on German merchant ships with anti-aircraft guns for protection and that traded with Sweden. When Germany was winning, they were treated with open arms; when they were losing, they had to dismantle their anti-aircraft guns and suffer restrictions and indignities in neutral ports.

Conclusion

An independent Ukraine was not an idea that sprang from the mixed population living there. It was espoused in the nineteenth-century Europe by the anti-Russia lobbies. Many prominent Poles participated in those efforts. After all, Chmielnicki and Mazepa were Poles. The actualisation of this idea was brought to life by Germany in WW1. Having pushed the Russian armies as far back as the river Don, they declared the area called the Ukraine a state. With prominent nationalists there, they made a treaty directed at the resurrecting Polish state on February 9, 1918 at Brest Litowsk. The Ukrainian state was politically and economically dependent on Germany as an antidote to the Polish state.

When Germany lost the war on the western front, it became obvious that this artificial, newly created state, despite the presence there of Austrian troops in which Ukrainian conscripts were serving, had no roots in the local population. When the revolutionary Red Army swept through all of Eastern Europe in 1920, up to the gates of Warsaw, where it was finally stopped by the Polish army and ultimately defeated and pushed back as far as Kiew, the land called the Ukraine became Polish again. After the defeat and total occupation of Poland by Germany in 1939, the Ukraine was considered by them as a fertile colony to be milked.

Only after the Stalingrad and Kursk defeats, the demand for gun fodder for the eastern front forced the creation of Ukrainian units.

A Ukrainian state can only exist with the help of Germany and is, therefore, hostile to Poland and Russia. It had no history, so its elites created one, glorifying cut-throat bands of the SS Galizien, the UPA, and other militants who carried out the ethnic cleansing. They claimed the achievements of other long-established nations. For example, prominent Polish writers, artists, and intellectuals are never mentioned as Poles in the Ukrainian press. Even worse, some are portrayed as Ukrainians. They have a complex culture created by the contact between Latin Polish culture and the culture associated with illiterate Ukrainian peasants.

The intelligent and informed reader sees a seasonal state— (a term used as a derogatory description of Poland by the German press after Germany's defeat at the western front in WW1) with unbelievable corruption, powerful foreign influences, and oligarchs—unable to defend itself without massive outside help. The German-created republic consists of two Ukraines. The first one is the Greek-Catholic, red-black-flagged western Ukraine, the Ukrainian population of which was and is hostile to anything Polish. The other is the blue-yellow Ukraine of the east, where there is little hostility. The problem with the western Ukraine today is that the nationalists were for the kaiser's and Hitler's Germany, whereas in the eastern Ukraine, they were under the cultural influence of Mother Russia.

Most of their western elites were trained in Germany for which they provided SS Galicien and other killers of the then majority Polish population to create a vassal state free of Poles, Jews, Russians, and others. The brutality of the "Ukrainian only" policy has not changed since the twentieth century. According to the July 6, 1995, *Herald Sun* (Australia), a Ukrainian man killed and skinned a woman.

Its previously elected president, Janukowycz, had good relations with Russia. This was against the policy of Germany, the EU, NATO, and the United States. Various foreign billionaires and local oligarchs poured money into the coffers of the west Ukrainian organisations descended from the SS Galizien, UPA, and others to topple the government. Among the donors were George Soros and local oligarchs, such as Poroszenko of the Roshen chocolate empire and a TV station and Pintschuk of the steel mills.

Transport, food, and tents were arranged under the leadership of professional agitators to proceed to Kiew for a mass rally to oust the president and bind the Ukraine to Germany as it was after WWI and during WWII. The mob, often wearing swastikas on their helmets and giving the Hitler salute, had arms delivered to them by the EU and forced the president to seek refuge in Russia. They installed their own president, who is subservient to the United States and Germany. Angela Merkel, the German prime minister, appointed a US citizen of Ukrainian descent as her finance minister to facilitate help and weapons for her new colony and long-time ally. Ban Ki-moon, the general secretary of the United Nations, made a statement on April 7, 2014, not repeated to the general public nor in Ukrainian media "As the Ukraine has not registered its borders as a sovereign state, there can be no violation by Russia of its territory." (novorus.info/news/events 16657). Today's Russia is the rightful heir of the former USSR and has inherited all the lands that were part of it. Therefore, the new not yet state should establish agreements regarding its borders with all neighbouring states, including today's Russia.

The mass media in Germany, the United States, and all colonies—including the previous government of Poland—welcomed the change of government there in order to annoy Russia. That government consisted of persons holding multiple passports. One prominent official is a member of the elite of a country whose signature is on the Yalta Agreement, where the latest partition of Poland was agreed on. Anglo-Saxon media never mention the SS Galizien nor the cutthroats of the UPA and other militias; it is as if they never existed. The massacre of the majority Polish population of the western Ukraine is never mentioned. Today, as in the past, Germany trains their officers and administrators and supplies armoured vehicles, other weapons, and money according to their century-old Drang nach Osten that, so far, has given New York banks control over the Baltics and Poland.

On July 17, 2014, a Malaysian passenger aicraft of the type Boeing 777 with 298 persons on board was shot down over the eastern Ukraine by a Buk-M1 weapon. As anyone conversant with military matters knows, when an army moves, some equipment, often in woking order, is for whatever reason, abandoned. Eastern Poland was the staging point for all kinds of millitary hardware during the cold war. Not all was removed after the collapse of the Soviet Union, and it was seized by whatever organised group filled the vaccum.. Of course, the United States and its faithful colonies of Germany and others and their mass media blamed Russian seperatists as they resent Russia being govened by President Putin, who puts the interests of his country first.

As a retired LAME (electronics) commercial pilot with some thirty years in aviation, I can assure the reader that only whoever first recovered a working voice and data recorder will know the truth. The same applies to the crash of the Polish aircraft at

Smolensk on April 10, 2010, with the president and original Solidarity members on board.

The loss of Poland's eastern territories cannot be tied with it accepting the regained lands in the west. The lands that belonged to Germany before WWII were lost by Germany as recompensation for its aggression of Poland and the holocaust of the flowers of the educated classes and patriotic citizenship starting in 1939. On the other hand, lands that belonged to Poland before WWII were lost when it became a victim of the Soviet-German pact and invasion. The loss of its eastern lands by Germany as an aggressor and destroyer of everything Polish is fair and justified. The betrayal by its allies is unjust and unlawful. The western lands Poland regained after centuries of German expansion; the Drang nach Osten has been stopped there. Its aim was the abolition of the Polish state, accomplished during the partitions in the eighteenth century and repeated in 1939. Extermination of the Polish-Latin cultures both in the east and west occurred hand-in-hand with the destruction of the state with the help of Lithuanian, Ukrainian, and Belorussian minorities.

The new government of the Ukraine has introduced the draft. There is little enthusiasm for it. Every second draftee is trying to avoid military service, and many make their way to the Russian side. The Crimea was always part of Russia, and right after the war, it was transferred administratively to the Ukrainian Peoples Republic, one of the many republics in the USSR.

Valentina Lisita, born in Kiew in 1973, is a well-known Ukrainian pianist, residing in North Carolina. She is also a well-known critic of past and present Ukrainian leadership. Her outspokenness earned her the enmity of the Ukrainian diaspora of former SS Galicjen, UPA, and other criminal organisations well settled there. She claims oligarchs always have power in the Ukraine.

To support their families at home, three million Ukrainians live and work in Russia. As another example of the conditions among the elite, before Jazeniuk became prime minister, he sold his eight-year-old Range Rover for $120 000 to Pawlo Petrenko, today the minister of justice. The real value of the Land Rover was $20 000.

Armament industries are delighted with the situation there. Lower-level officials pocket bribes from those unwilling to do compulsory military service. Both sides in the internal conflict use mercenaries. The coal mines and factories of the oligarch Achmedow are not attacked by any side as both are provided financial help. The former commander of the Asov battalions that were as cruel as the SS Galicien has recently been appointed police chief of Kiew.

Ukraine's trade partners, however, are upset. China bought wheat, paid **1.5** million US dollars in advance but got only 10 per cent of the promised amount. In addition, 1.5 million was provided for projects, but nobody knows where the money went. The EU gave millions to secure the borders. A considerable amount of these monies vanished without a trace.

History is not concerned with daily matters but deals in centuries and millenniums. Those who have carved up Poland and benefited from their betrayal of Poland will lose one day what they have stolen. Three foreign citizens were appointed ministers in the previous government. To those who have made it a colony of foreign, treacherous empires, I say study the Polish national anthem, which contains the words, "What foreign power has taken away from us with the sword we will reclaim." It might take centuries, but the day will come when the evil empires of this world will collapse, and those that have benefited by the loss of Poland's eastern lands will lose their ill-gotten gains.

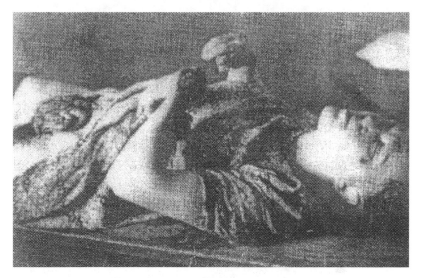

Woman victim of Ukrainian atrocity.
Copyright by Norton publisher, Wroclaw, Poland.

Lithuania

In 1914, at the beginning of W W I, the geographical area called Lithuania and eastern Poland were parts of the Russian empire under the czar. The ancient and principal city in the Lithuanian area was Wilno. Its majority population was Polish, with a great number of Jews and other nationalities. In 1917, the Lithuanian population in Wilno was only 2 per cent (German statistics).

When the czar's empire collapsed due to its defeat by Germany/ Austria and the Bolschewik Revolution in 1917, many of the minority nationalities of that empire attempted to form their own states. The Bolsheviks, after winning the civil war in Russia, sent their armies in 1920 westwards across these lands to aid the Bolshevik revolution in defeated Germany. They handed Wilno and surrounding lands to Lithuania as a reward for its assistance in the war with Poland.

Soon after, Lithuania became one of the many Soviet republics. Their political leaders escaped to Germany, its friend and mentor. In Berlin, they immediately set up their organisation under the name Lithuanian Activists Front. The new masters of those lands organised the deportation of some thirty thousand Poles to Siberia with the cooperation of the Lithuanian minority. Resurrected Poland, after 150 years of foreign occupation by the Russian, German, and Austrian empires, stopped the red hordes at the gates of Warsaw and reclaimed its ancient city of Wilno. The peace treaty was signed by both parties at Riga (Latvia).

In the following peaceful years, Wilno and the surrounding districts, an area of 6,680 sq.km had 441,100 inhabitants. Of those, 31,300 were Lithuanians. There were 217,000 Poles, 107,600 Jews, 75,200 Belorussians, 9,900 Russians, and some others. The city itself had a population consisting of Poles (70 per cent), Jews (29 per cent), and Lithuanians (0.07 per cent).

In 1939, when Germany invaded Poland, the Wilno region was again annexed by the Soviet Union. From 1939 until the collapse of the USSR, the Poles of the Wilno region had two ruthless occupiers and persecutors. An enforced program of Lithuanisation of the majority Polish population was again instituted by all authorities with the full cooperation of the Lithuanian population.

This continues to this day. In 1941, Hitler's armies turned against their erstwhile allies, and German troops entered Wilno greeted by Lithuanian women in their native costumes with flowers.

General Krzyzanowski, Wilno region, January 1944 (in public domain).

Lithuanian volunteers formed *Sonderkommandos* to carry out the ethnic cleansing of the newly acquired land of Poles, Jews, Soviet POWs, and Roma. Poles were evicted from the land they toiled for centuries and their property given for nothing to Lithuanian peasants. A Lithuanian priest of the parish of Jeczmienieszki assisted in the eviction of the Polish owners. The Lithuanian Catholic clergy's persecution of their Catholic Polish brothers is unique in the history of the Catholic Church. It proves that their Christian religion for them is for show only. Underneath is the primitive and barbaric heathen. During Soviet occupation, deep, concrete-reinforced trenches were built in Ponary, an area covered by forests. These trenches were built to house a future fuel depot for a planned nearby airfield. German occupiers and their Lithuanian helpers deemed it to be suitable for a mass grave of the victims of their ethnic cleansing. There they executed some 100,000 citizens of pre-war Poland, 70,000 Jews, and 20,000 Poles, Russians,

Roma, and Lithuanian communists. All of the Poles were shot, according to lists already prepared by Lithuanian activists, with emphasis on the educated. They were shot naked, their clothing and boots taken by a Lithuanian trader whose brother assisted in the executions. Polish student youth, both male and female, were singled out to be eliminated. The public service was purged of Poles and persons of Polish descent. In Kowno, 3,800 Jews were executed under the leadership of Agirdas Klimaitis, Colonel Kazys Simkus, and Lieutenant Bronius Norkus. In the surrounding provinces, 1,200 were killed, mostly wealthier Jews in order to loot their property. In Wilno, starting on July 11, 1941, a unit of the Yapatingasis Burys (called Ponarian rifles) cleaned the city of Poles, Jews, and Russians. A German *Sonderkommando3/a,* under the command of SS-Obersturmfuhrer Hammann is credited with the killing of 137,000. This unit had some eighty Lithuanian activists. The perpetrators were the Lithuanian criminal police, which was on par with the German gestapo. I personally witnessed a group of Lithuanian policemen in German police uniforms with the inscription *Litauen,* strutting masterly in a Polish city. Fifty Poles were executed on May 5. The next day, they executed Father Swirkowski, a Catholic priest. Between the ninth and seventeenth of May, eighty were executed, including some high school students.

The priest in charge of the Jeczmieniszki parish, Father Ambrazicjus Jakowonis, collaborated with the gestapo and Saguna organisations. When his collaboration was discovered, he was found guilty by the AK military court and executed.

In June and July 1941, a special unit of the *Sicherheitspolizei* and *Sicherheitsdienst,* under the Lithuanian name of "Sontingas Burys," was formed and led by professional pre-war officers of the Lithuanian army. The unit wore German police uniforms, and from 1942 onward, carried out executions at Ponary. Other locations where executions were carried out were Niemenczyn, Nowa, Wilejka, Orany, Jaszuny, Troki, and Swieciany. The Lithuanian security police, Saugumo, was reconstructed from the time of the German occupation. They used a considerable number of informers to penetrate any clandestine organisations, Polish, and others opposed to the Reich.

Soldiers of the AK on the streets of Wilno, 1944 (in public domain).

At the order of the chief of the Lithuanian police, Antanas Iskauskas, an internment camp for Polish priests was set up at Saltupe. Into that camp were forced 15 professors from a seminary attached to the St. George Church in Wilno and 250 brothers from a monastic order.

Only late in the war, 1943–1944, after the Polish AK and NSZ gained in strength in those areas, was the plague of Lithuanian informers curtailed. Inspector Marianas Padabas of the Lithuanian police was responsible for the deaths of many young Poles. He was convicted by a AK court and shot in Wilno on August 15, 1943. Some Lithuanian Catholic priests collaborated with the informers.

The priest attached to the central jail in Wilno, Bartomajtys, informed the Saugumo and gestapo of any information obtained during confession. The local bishop, Reinys, was aware of his activities.

Lithuanian police battalions, Apsaugos Battalion—or *Schutzmannschaftbattalione* in German—consisted of political activists. They provided security to radio stations and magazines, and guards for POW camps and Jewish ghettos. In 1942, they numbered 8,400 men, 341 officers, and 1772 NCOs. These units were also used in the territories of other occupied Soviet republics and the Majdanek concentration camp in occupied Poland. They took part in the liquidation of the Warsaw Ghetto. In the Polish township of Swienciny, in May the 19 and 20, 450 Poles were executed. A recruiting drive for people to work in Germany was started in May 1942. Lithuanian administration ensured that 22,000 Poles were selected for this task.

When in January 1943 the situation on the eastern front deteriorated, it was suggested that a Lithuanian legion of the Waffen SS could be formed. SS Brigardenfuhrer Wysocki conducted talks to that effect with Lithuanian colonel Antanas Reklatis and proposed the colonel take charge, but he refused. Only some two hundred volunteered, and that plan was abandoned. When the Red Army was at the gates of Wilno in June 1944, the leadership of the Polish AK under General Krzyzanowski decided to oust the German forces so that the town would be deemed to be liberated by them. An action under the name of *Ostra Brama* was undertaken on June 26, with only partial success with twelve thousand men, and the white/red flag was hoisted atop the town hall. It was promptly removed and replaced with the red flag by the Red Army. Losses to the Poles were heavy as the Germans with eighteen thousand men had fortified important positions and had some knowledge of the impending Polish action, heavy weapons, and air support. The AK soldiers were arrested and deported to the Siberian gulag.

A considerable number of Lithuanian volunteers joined the German Wehrmacht. The one I met on the way to Australia boasted that he served in the Africa Corps. Every government of Lithuania, whether dependent on the goodwill of one occupier or another, has continued the process of compulsory lithuanisation. The disposition of land owned by Poles was confiscated under some manufactured pretext or other, and the settlement thereon of inhabitants of Lithuania proper has been going on for years. Government officials of all shades do not negotiate with clients in their language as they do in Australia. Today, both countries are signatories to the UN convention, protecting minorities, but Lithuania simply ignores it. In June 1944, thirty-nine Poles, including children and the old, were executed in the villages of Gilincziszki and Dubinki on the order of Lieutenant Petras Polekauskas. He survived the war and settled in the United States. In most cases, the names of the killers were known, yet they escaped justice.

Lithuanian authorities then and now follow their much-admired German Reich in dealing with minorities. In Australia, translations of administrative laws and regulations are also in languages of the various minorities living there. On official documents in today's Lithuania the endings of names are changed to sound Lithuanian. Historical achievers in literature, the sciences, and so on of other nations are claimed as Lithuanian. All this shows that an unimportant minority in any country can become ultimately a majority using Hitler's methods and the support of a major power. It is the classic Bismarckian *Kulturkampf.* As an example of what kind of people the Lithuanians earmarked for destruction let me quote the qualifications of one of their victims, Dr. Kazimiez Pelczar. An outstanding medical authority on cancer, trained at Jagielon University of Cracow, universities of Berlin and Paris. He had the opportunity to escape to London, which he declined. His usefulness to the Lithuanians could not be questioned. However, their hatred of everything Polish exceeded their common sense. Being nominally Catholics, they behaved then and now as unthinking heathens. Protests to the UN or any other world organisation are a waste of time and resources as these organisations are no more than toothless tigers. The Lithuanian minister of defence, Juozasa Olekasa, confirmed his country's admiration of all Germany's leaders and their methods of dealing with minorities from Bismarck to Hitler with the words, "the Germans understand our concern as to the safety of our country and are [and were in WWII] faithful allies of Lithuania."

The knowledge of the ethnic cleansing of Lithuania by Lithuanians is never mentioned there nor anywhere else. Not even by any authorities of the previous government in today's Poland as those who ruled the country then by the grace of the United States and the EU were themselves (or their offspring) guilty of the crime of Cain. The mass media of the West and those of the Vatican do not mention it, of course, as they do not want their lemmings to know the truth. On the international scene, small, weak nations are the ideal clients of greater powers because they can easily be manipulated. Goebbels, Hitler's propaganda minister, was in favour of this method. To divide a potential opponent into a number of small countries has been the favourite method of larger countries. That is why Germany has always favoured and supported Ukrainian and Lithuanian minorities on Poland's land.

Glossary

The Ukraine

Hetman = Leader of a Cossack tribe
Tzar = Emperor of all Russians
Bolshevik army = Red Army

Abwehr = Hitler's military intelligence under Admiral Canaris
OUN = Organisation of Ukrainian Nationalists
Motorum motivabum = Cause of action
Wehmacht = German army
Waffen SS = Political soldiers
Anders = Polish officer jailed in the Lubianka NKVD prison, Moscow
Ostarbeiter = Forced or volunteer worker from USSR
De facto = In fact
Sonderkommando = Special unit
Bona fide = Real

Lithuania

Saguna = Secret police
Sicherheitsdienst = Security service
Sicherheitspolizei = Security police
Crime of Cain = In the Bible Old Testament, Cain killed his brother.

Ostra Brama = "Sharp gate"; an ancient gate with a famous religious painting and chapel; a place of pilgrimage in Wilno

Printed in the United States
By Bookmasters